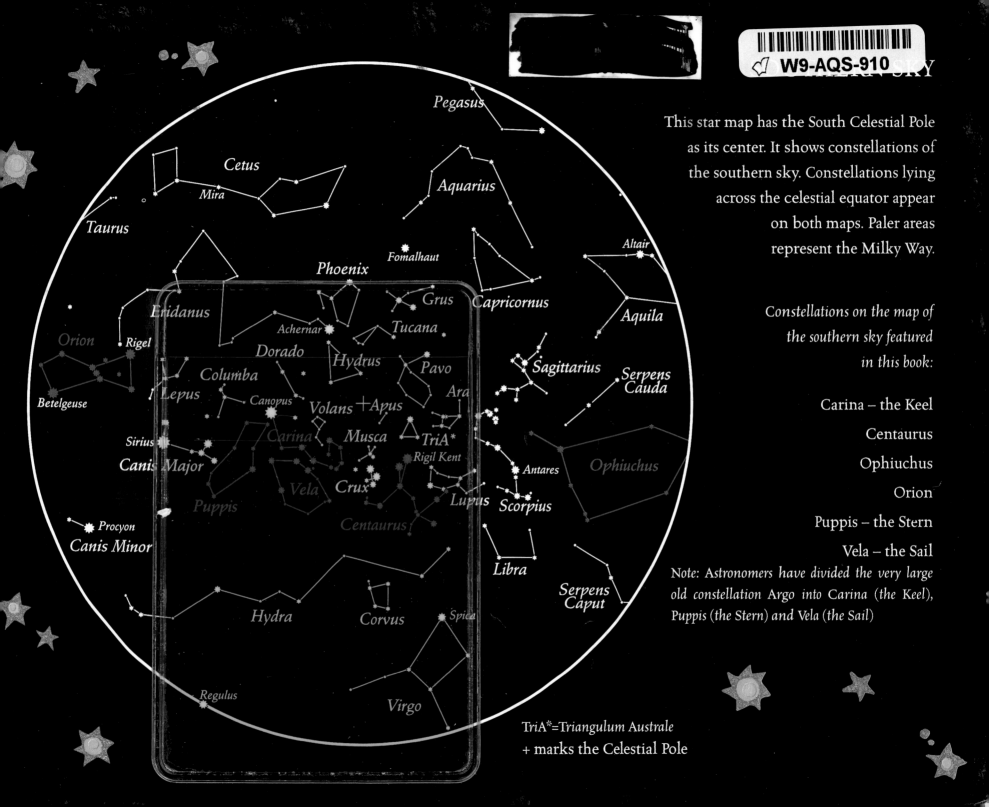

SKY

This star map has the South Celestial Pole as its center. It shows constellations of the southern sky. Constellations lying across the celestial equator appear on both maps. Paler areas represent the Milky Way.

Constellations on the map of the southern sky featured in this book:

Carina – the Keel

Centaurus

Ophiuchus

Orion

Puppis – the Stern

Vela – the Sail

Note: Astronomers have divided the very large old constellation Argo into Carina (the Keel), Puppis (the Stern) and Vela (the Sail)

Pegasus

Cetus

Mira

Taurus

Aquarius

Phoenix

Fomalhaut

Altair

Eridanus

Grus

Capricornus

Aquila

Orion

Rigel

Achernar

Tucana

Dorado

Hydrus

Pavo

Sagittarius

Serpens Cauda

Betelgeuse

Columba

Canopus

Volans +Apus

Ara

Lepus

Musca

TriA*

Sirius

Carina

Rigil Kent

Ophiuchus

Canis Major

Vela

Crux

Antares

Puppis

Centaurus

Lupus

Scorpius

Procyon

Canis Minor

Libra

Serpens Caput

Hydra

Corvus

Spica

Regulus

Virgo

TriA*=Triangulum Australe

+ marks the Celestial Pole

FOR SIMON – J.M.

FOR MY SISTERS AMIRA AND DANNI – C.B.

First American edition

First published in Great Britain in 2003 by Frances Lincoln Limited,
4 Torriano Mews, Torriano Avenue, London NW5 2RZ
www.franceslincoln.com

Published by the National Geographic Society.

ISBN 0-7922-6332-4

One of the world's largest nonprofit scientific and educational organizations, the National Geographic Society
was founded in 1888 "for the increase and diffusion of geographic
knowledge." Fulfilling this mission, the Society educates and inspires millions every day through
its magazines, books, television programs, videos, maps and atlases, research grants, the National Geographic
Bee, teacher workshops, and innovative classroom materials. The Society is supported through membership
dues, charitable gifts, and income from the sale of its educational products.
This support is vital to National Geographic's mission to increase global understanding and
promote conservation of our planet through exploration, research, and education.
For more information, please call 1-800-NGS LINE (647-5463) or write to the following address:

NATIONAL GEOGRAPHIC SOCIETY.
1145 17th Street N.W.
Washington, D.C. 20036-4688 U.S.A.
Visit the Society's Web site: www.nationalgeographic.com

Library of Congress Cataloguing in Publication Data available on request

Printed in Hong Kong
9 8 7 6 5 4 3 2 1

Once Upon a Starry Night

A Book of Constellations

Jacqueline Mitton

✳

Christina Balit

NATIONAL
GEOGRAPHIC

WASHINGTON, D.C.

THE LAST HINTS of pink and orange have faded in the west. Darkness creeps across the clear sky like a velvet curtain. It's a perfect night for telling a story.

But what about some pictures to go with the story? Look up, and what do you see? Not just stars, but a vast picture book. The night sky is a realm of kings and queens, gods, heroes, and mystical creatures. Look—they're all there, outlined by the stars. You only need a little imagination....

CASSIOPEIA

Where the Milky Way tumbles through the northern sky sits Queen Cassiopeia, a zigzag of dazzling stars, with Cepheus, her king, close by.

"See how beautiful I am," she declared one day, "fairer than all the nymphs of the sea."

Poseidon was angry with Cassiopeia. "No mortal insults my nymphs!" said the ocean god. "I'll punish you for your vanity." And he sent a frightful sea monster to terrify the kingdom.

ANDROMEDA

Andromeda is King Cepheus's beloved daughter. A spiral galaxy lies just beside her, and the blue and yellow gem of a double star flashes on her skirt.

"Sacrifice your daughter—it's the only way to stop the beast," her father was told. So the princess was chained to rocks by the sea to await her horrible fate.

Her heart beat fast with fear. Would anyone help her before it was too late?

PERSEUS

Perseus to the rescue! Winged sandals on his feet, the hero speeds through the Milky Way to Andromeda's side. He carries the fearsome head of Medusa, the ghastly Gorgon he has slain. The Demon Star that is Medusa's eye winks eerily. Perseus holds high his magic sickle, twin star clusters glistening beside his hand.

"Death to the sea monster!" he cries.

So Andromeda was saved, and bold Perseus married his princess.

PEGASUS

Pegasus the heavenly horse soars gracefully overhead, four bright stars at the corners of his Great Square.

After Perseus had killed Medusa, Pegasus sprang up where her blood had fallen. Faithfully the winged horse served the mighty god Zeus, carrying his thunder and lightning.

When the mortal Bellopheron mounted Pegasus and tried to ride him to the realm of the gods, angry Zeus flung him back to Earth—but rewarded Pegasus for his loyal service by setting him in the stars.

LYRA

High in the sky, a great bird bears the lyre of Orpheus, adorned with bright stars and a wispy ring of gleaming gas.

Orpheus's singing left his listeners spellbound, and the music of his lyre held them like a charm.

Grief stricken after his young wife died, he softened the hearts of the underworld gods with his music.

"Your wife may follow you to the land of the living," they decreed, "so long as you do not look at her on the way." But Orpheus couldn't resist glancing back—and she was gone forever.

HERCULES

Immortalized by the gods, Hercules the superhero kneels in the sky, a clustering ball of stars at his thigh.

Renowned for his many feats of strength, Hercules (called Herakles by the ancient Greeks) could not be harmed by sword or fire because of the miraculous lion skin he wore. He didn't fear the fiery dragon who guarded the golden apples of the Hesperides. For one of his famous labors he seized the apples—and crushed the dragon with his foot!

ORION

Striding boldly through the heavens comes the brilliant hunter Orion.

Son of the sea-god Poseidon, he could walk on water and was tall enough to wade through the ocean. So great a huntsman was this handsome giant, even the goddess Artemis deigned to hunt with him. But when he dared to touch her, Artemis was furious and her punishment speedy: Orion died from a scorpion's sting.

Now starry pearls stud his belt, and where his sword hangs, a haze of glowing gas glistens.

CENTAURUS

Chiron the Centaur—half-man, half-horse—trots along the Milky Way.

Clever and kind, wise and fair, immortal Chiron was a wonderful teacher and healer. Then, by chance, a poisoned arrow struck him, and there was no cure.

"This pain is too great to bear forever," he cried. He begged to die, and Zeus granted his wish, giving him an honored place in the sky.

Now a fuzzy swarm of a million stars rides on the Centaur's back. Our nearest bright star, Alpha Centauri, burns yellow at his foot.

OPHIUCHUS

Is it dangerous to hold a snake?

"I'm not afraid. This snake has healing powers," says the serpent-holder Ophiuchus. This heavenly figure is the god of medicine whom the ancient Greeks called Asclepius.

With his magical skills, Asclepius could even bring the dead back to life – but this made Zeus frown.

"No god should meddle with life and death in the world of mortals," he cried. Raising his thunderbolt, the king of the gods struck Asclepius down, but afterward placed him among the stars.

ARGO

"**B**ring me the sacred golden Fleece!" commanded Jason's scheming uncle (secretly thinking, "He'll die if he tries.") But undeterred, Jason and fifty friends set off in the great ship *Argo* on their dangerous adventure.

"To win the Fleece, first yoke my fiery bulls and sow these dragon's teeth," demanded the king who owned the Fleece. "Then fight the soldiers who spring up where the teeth fall." Impossible? No! With magical help, Jason won the Fleece.

Now the *Argo* sails a sea of stars as three constellations: keel, stern, and sail.

STARS, NEBULAE, AND GALAXIES

The stars are like our Sun: huge balls of glowing gas. They look like small specks of light only because they are very far away. Some of the specks we see shining in the night sky look fuzzy. They are often called "nebulae"—from the Latin word for clouds. But there are several different kinds of fuzzy objects. Some really are bright clouds of gas; others are families of stars. You can tell the difference when you look at them through a telescope.

We are in the Milky Way galaxy, made up of thousands of millions of stars: All the stars we see belong to it. Our galaxy is shaped like a disc with a bulge in the middle and spiral arms winding out from the bulge. It is a great island of stars in space and just one of billions of galaxies in the universe. The band of light we see in the night sky is also called the Milky Way. It is the light of many distant stars.

CONSTELLATIONS

The stars in a constellation look near to each other in the sky, but they are not really close together: They are scattered in space, all at different distances from us. When we say that a star is "in a constellation," we are talking about where to find it in the sky, not where it is in space.

The whole sky is divided up between 88 different-size constellations, just as a continent is divided into countries or states. Every star, star cluster, nebula, or galaxy belongs to one of the constellations. The official names of constellations are in Latin, though some come from characters in Greek myths. This book uses the official constellation names as titles and the Greek names for the gods and goddesses who are in the stories.

MORE ABOUT SOME NIGHT SKY OBJECTS IN THIS BOOK

ANDROMEDA

The spiral galaxy in Andromeda is the most distant thing you can see without a telescope and the nearest large galaxy to our own. It is more than 2 million light-years away, which means that the light we pick up from it now set out from the galaxy more than 2 million years ago. Our Milky Way galaxy is similar to the Andromeda galaxy, but not quite as large.

PERSEUS

The second brightest star in Perseus is called Algol, or the Demon Star. Like clockwork, every 2 days 20 hours and 49 minutes, it dims noticeably, then brightens again. In reality, Algol is a pair of stars circling each other. Normally we see their combined light, but when the fainter star crosses in front of the brighter one, the pair looks fainter.

In Perseus you can also see the famous double star cluster, visible without a telescope. The two clusters are almost twins, and only about 50 light years apart, although more than 7,000 light-years away.

LYRA

Stars don't stay the same forever. They can last billions of years, but when they grow old, they change. In Lyra, there's an old star that swelled up into a giant, then puffed off its outside, like a shell, about 7,000 years ago. It formed a nebula called the Ring Nebula around what is left of the old star. You need a telescope to see it.

HERCULES

Some of the oldest stars in our galaxy can be found in tight, ball-shaped swarms of stars that astronomers call globular clusters. In Hercules you will find the brightest globular cluster in the northern half of the sky. Known simply as M13, it has no other name. About 300,000 stars are packed in this cluster, which is more than 20,000 light-years away. You can see it without a telescope.

ORION

Glowing gas around a group of bright young stars forms the famous Orion Nebula in the hunter's sword. Behind the nebula lurks a huge dark cloud of gas and dust 1,300 light-years away. This is a birthplace of stars. No more than a hundred thousand years ago, the stars in the Orion Nebula began to shine, blasting through the dark cloud with their rays and lighting up the gas around them. The nebula is visible without a telescope.

CENTAURUS

Centaurus is home to the brightest and biggest of all globular star clusters. Called Omega Centauri, it is 16,500 light-years away and 620 light-years across. You can easily see it without a telescope.

The brightest star in this constellation, Alpha Centauri, is the nearest bright star to the Sun, just over 4 light-years away. In reality it is a double star. The two stars slowly waltz around each other once every 80 years. A very dim star in Centaurus called Proxima is a tiny bit nearer to us than Alpha.

ARGO

The huge southern constellation Argo Navis (the ship *Argo*) existed for about 2,000 years. Then, in 1930, it was officially split into three when astronomers agreed to divide up the sky into 88 constellations. The parts of Argo are Carina (the Keel), Puppis (the Stern), and Vela (the Sail). But long before 1930, astronomers had been using these names for the different parts of Argo. The star Canopus, the brightest in Carina, is the second brightest in the whole sky. Also in Carina lies a lovely, brilliant cluster of 30 newly-formed stars, quite different from the old globular clusters. Although the cluster doesn't have a special name, it's easy to see without a telescope.

NORTHERN SKY

This star map has the North Celestial Pole as its center. It shows constellations of the northern sky. Constellations lying across the celestial equator appear on both maps. Paler areas represent the Milky Way.

Constellations on the map of the northern sky featured in this book:

Andromeda

Cassiopeia

Cepheus

Hercules

Lyra – the Lyre

Ophiuchus

Orion

Pegasus

Perseus

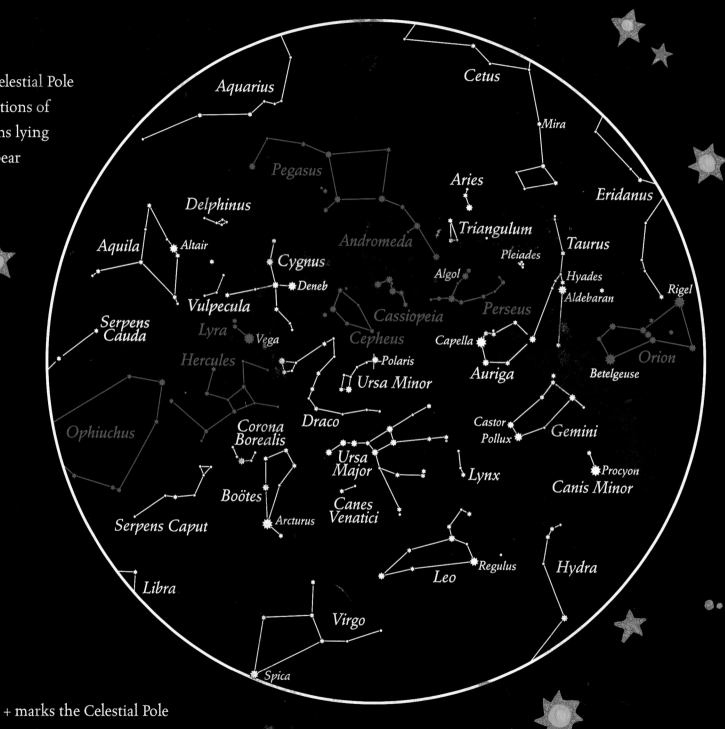

+ marks the Celestial Pole